A COLLECTION OF

HERMAN®
COLOR COMICS

by JIM Unger

Andrews and McMeel, Inc.
A Universal Press Syndicate Company
Kansas City • New York

HERMAN® is syndicated internationally by Universal Press Syndicate.

Herman Color Comics copyright © 1983 by Universal Press Syndicate. All rights reserved. Printed in the United States of America. No part of this book may be used or reproduced in any manner without written permission except in the case of reprints in the context of reviews. For information write Andrews and McMeel, Inc., a Universal Press Syndicate Company, 4400 Johnson Drive, Fairway, Kansas 66205.

ISBN: 0-8362-1216-9

Library of Congress Catalog Card Number: 83-71754

October 11, 1981

October 25, 1981

November 1, 1981

November 8, 1981

November 15, 1981

November 22, 1981

November 29, 1981

December 6, 1981

December 13, 1981

December 27, 1981

January 3, 1982

January 10, 1982

January 24, 1982

January 31, 1982

February 14, 1982

February 21, 1982

February 28, 1982

March 14, 1982

March 21, 1982

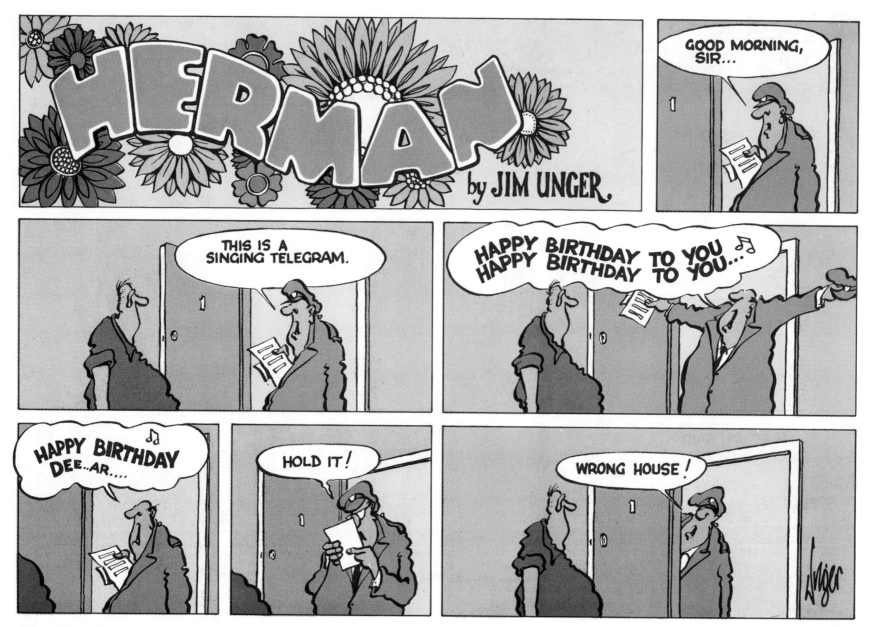

March 28, 1982

April 4, 1982

April 11, 1982

April 18, 1982

April 25, 1982

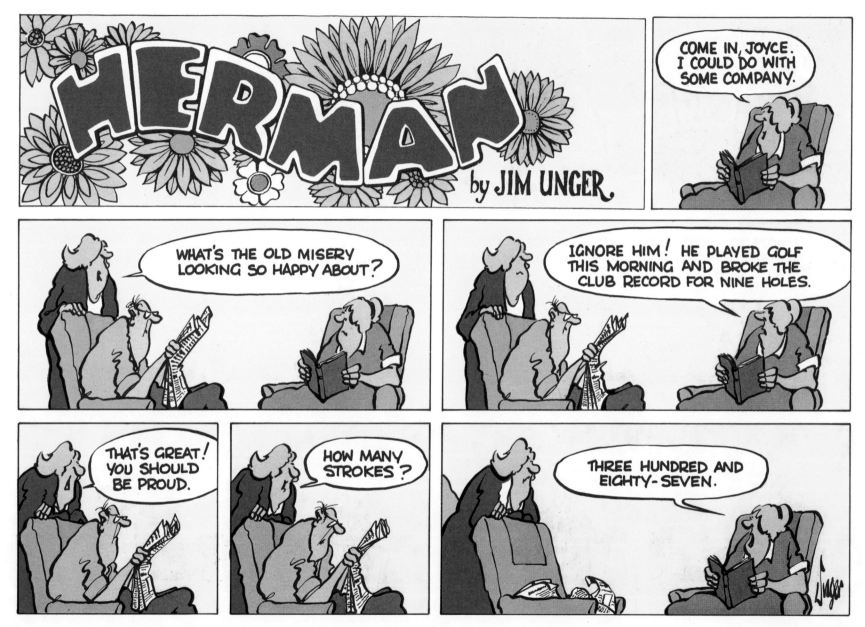

May 2, 1982

May 9, 1982

May 23, 1982

May 30, 1982

June 6, 1982

June 13, 1982

June 27, 1982

July 4, 1982

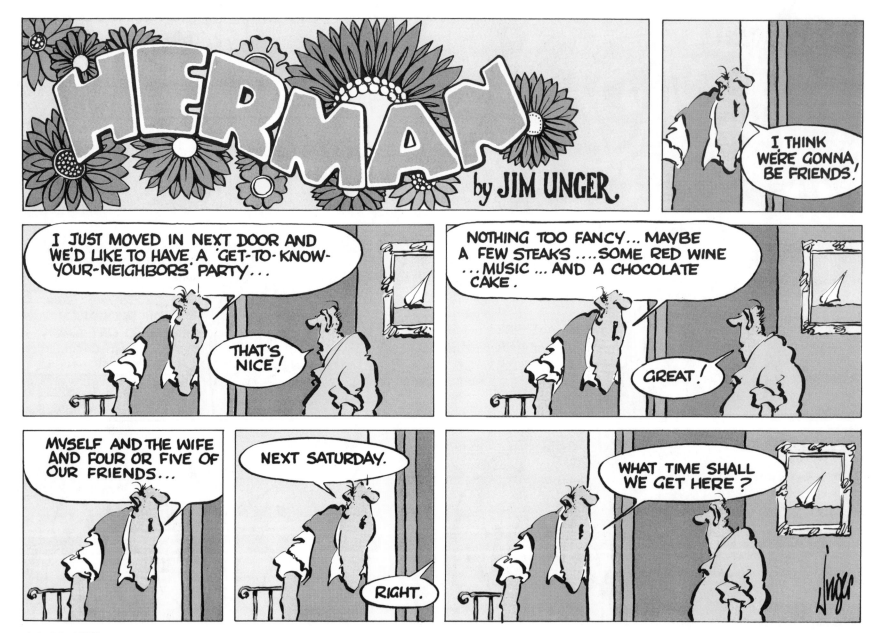

July 11, 1982

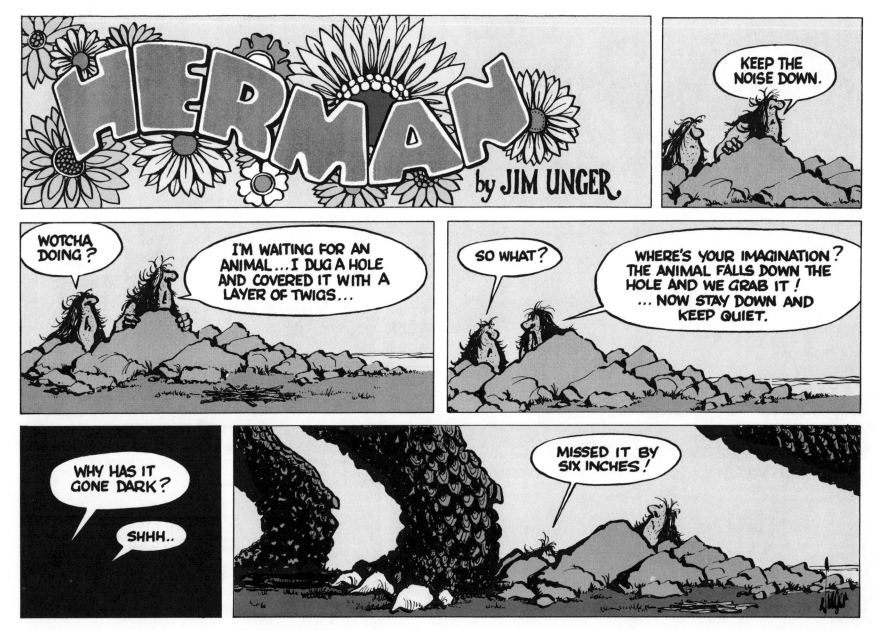

August 1, 1982

August 8, 1982

August 22, 1982

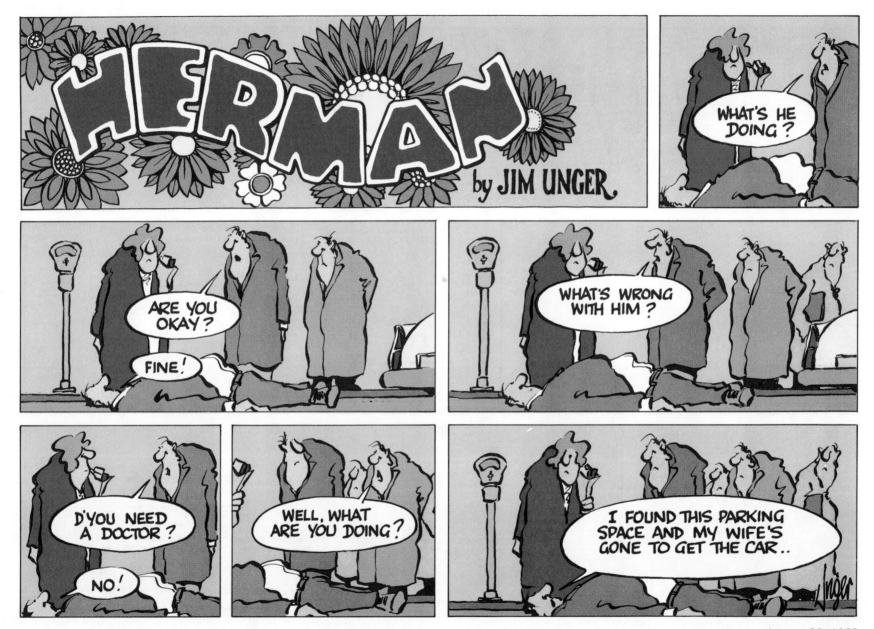

August 29, 1982

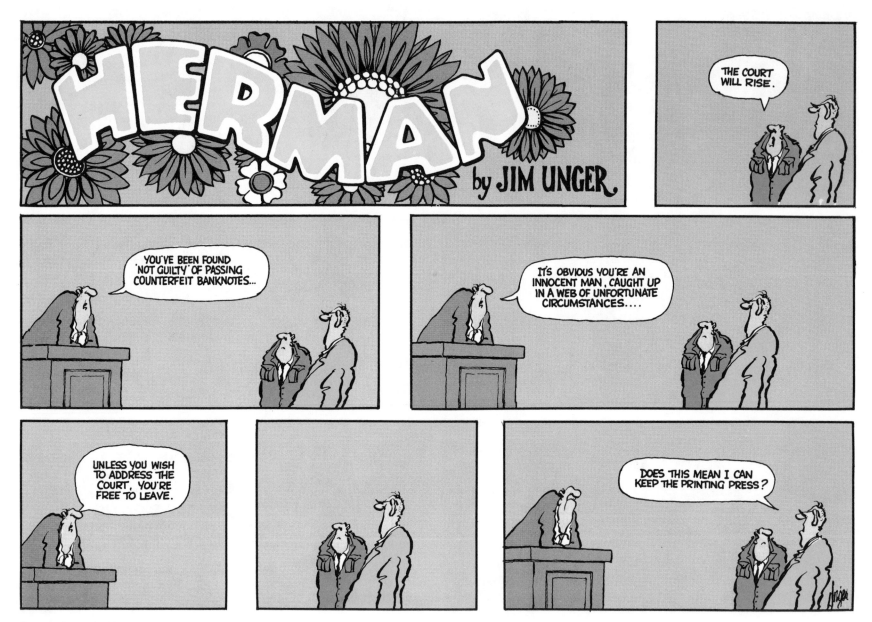

September 12, 1982

October 3, 1982

October 10, 1982

October 17, 1982

October 24, 1982

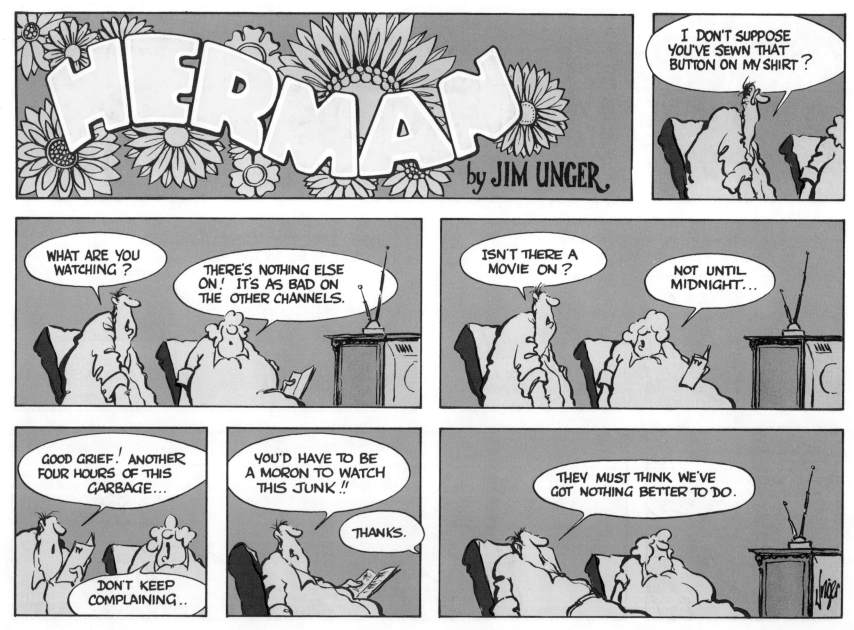

October 31, 1982

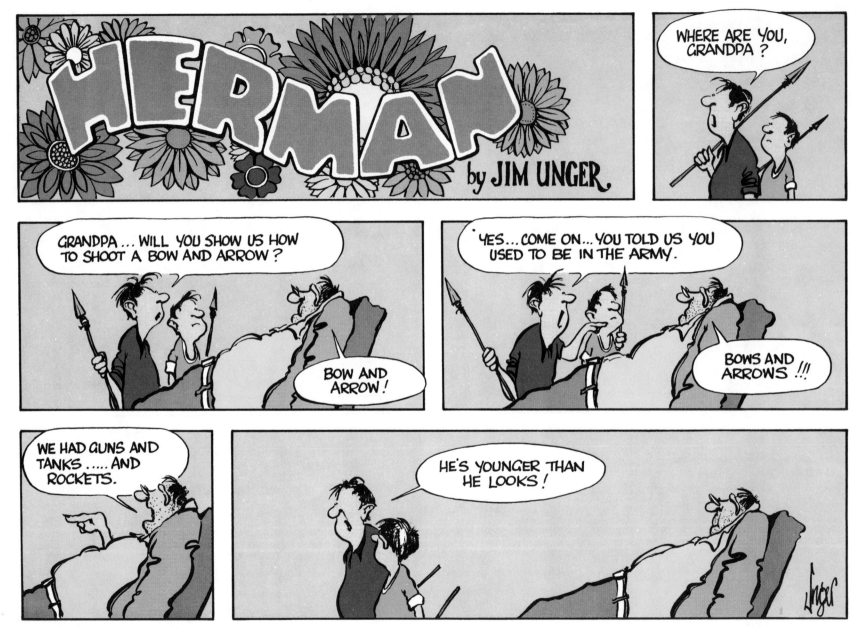

November 7, 1982

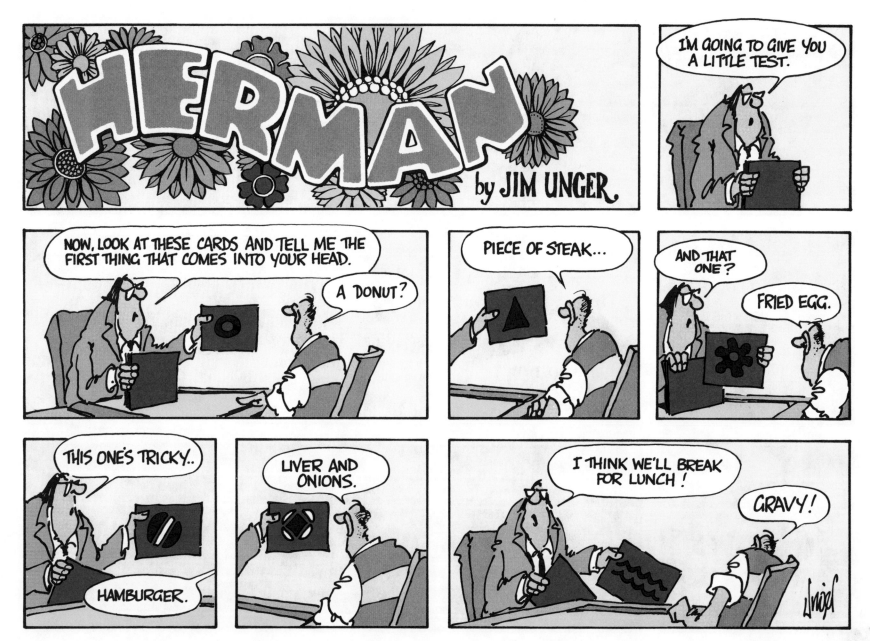

November 14, 1982

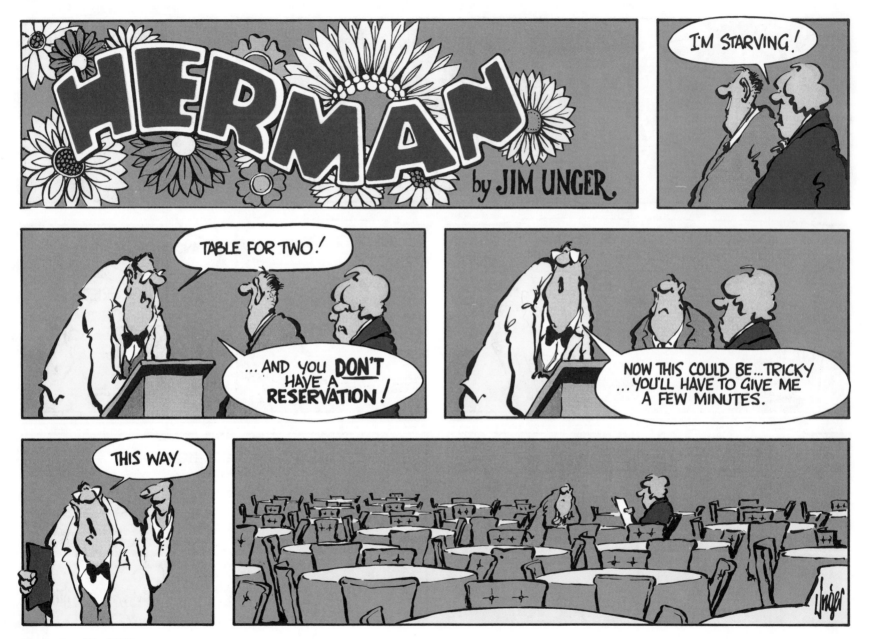

November 21, 1982

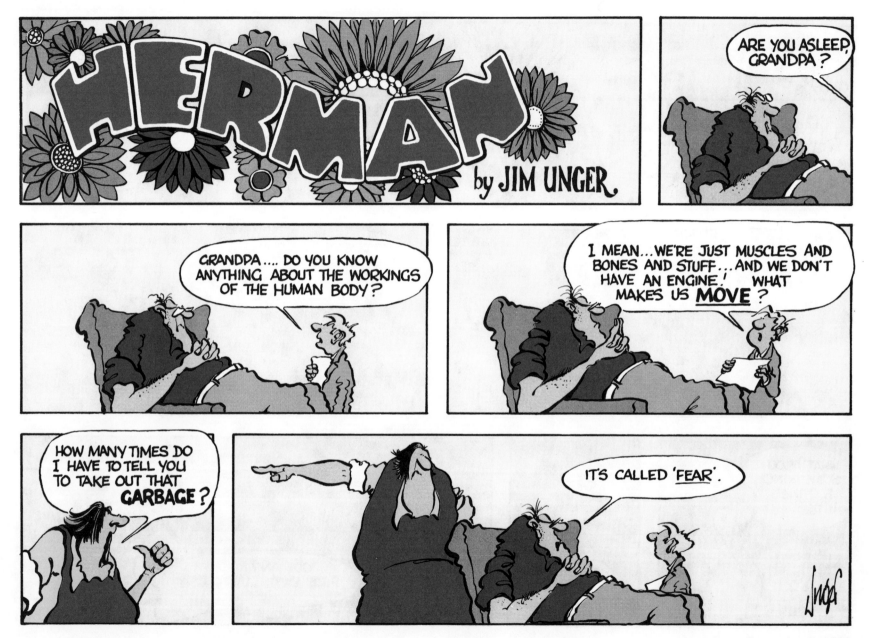

December 5, 1982

December 19, 1982

December 26, 1982

January 2, 1983

January 16, 1983

January 23, 1983

January 30, 1983

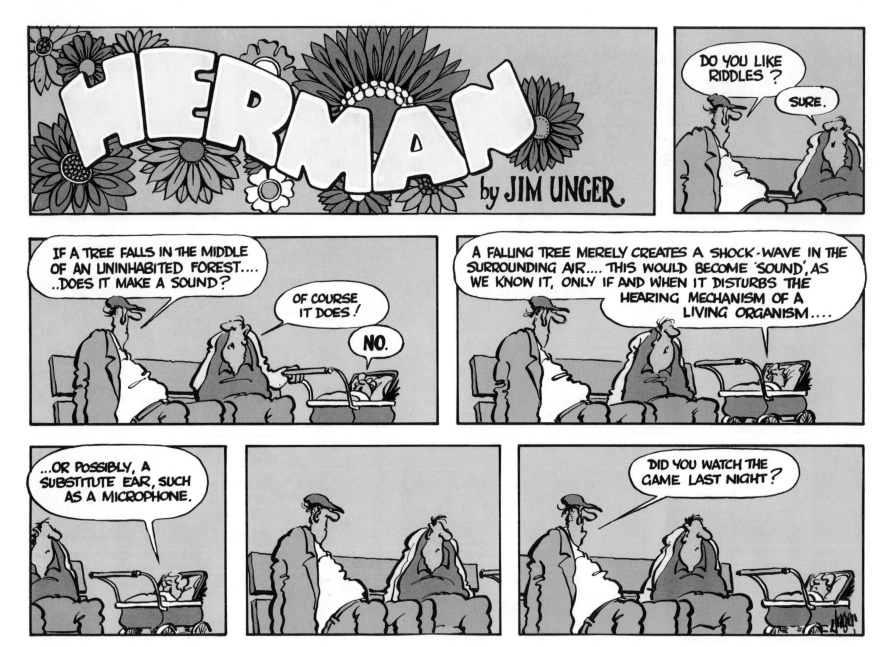

February 13, 1983

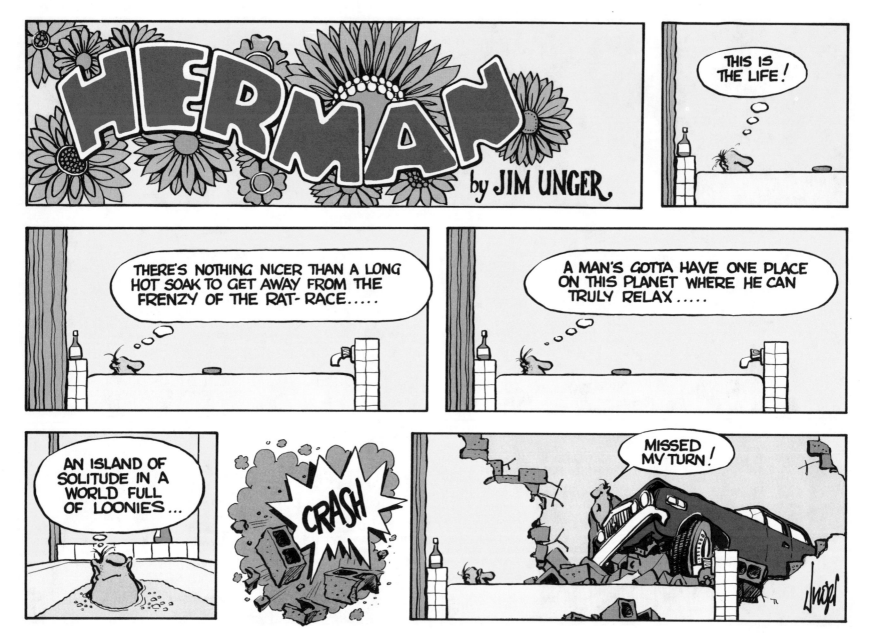

February 20, 1983

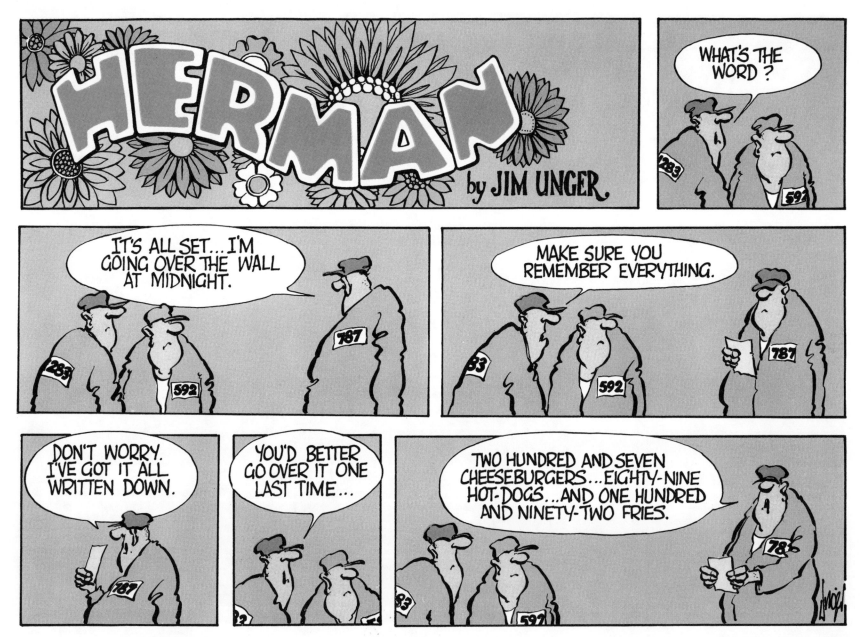

February 27, 1983

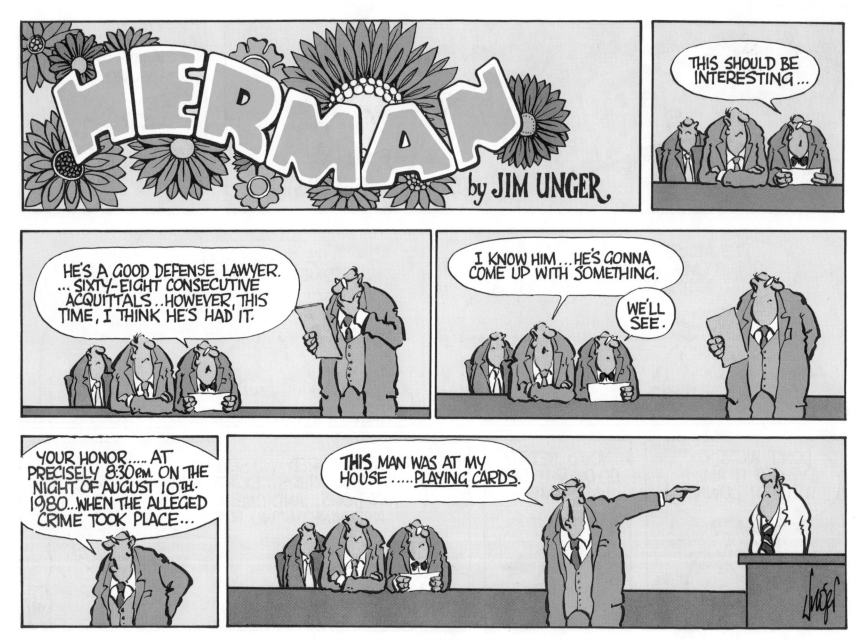

March 6, 1983

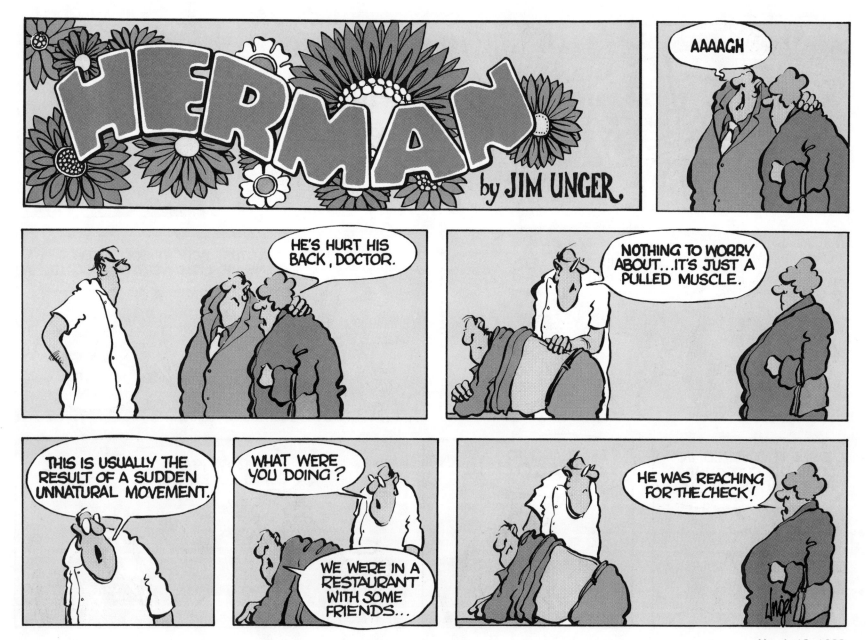

March 13, 1983

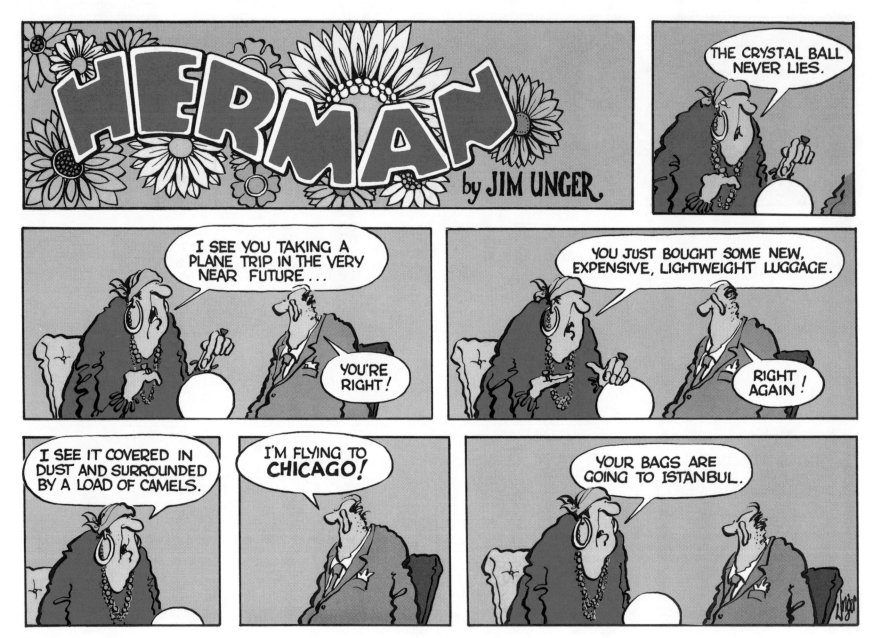

March 20, 1983

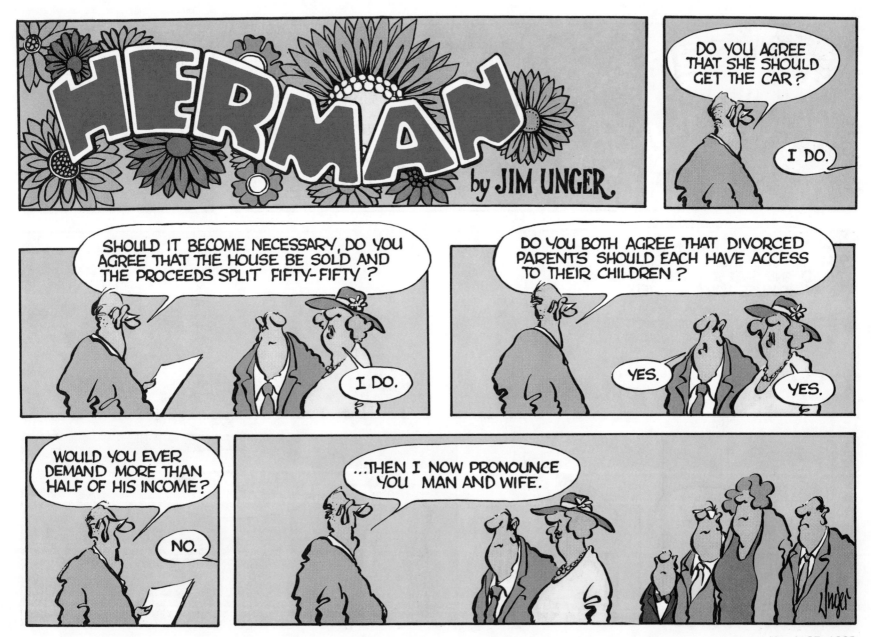

March 27, 1983

April 3, 1983

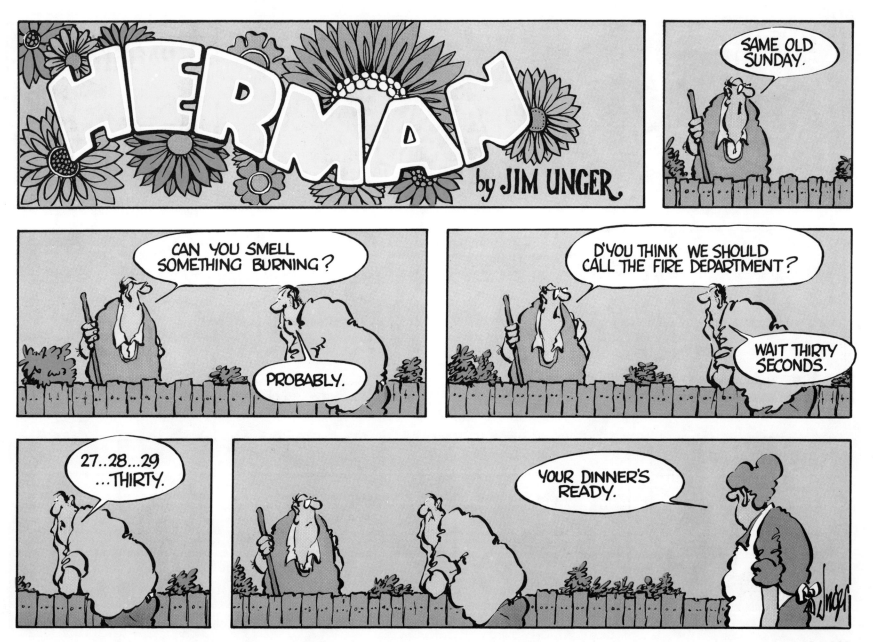

April 10, 1983

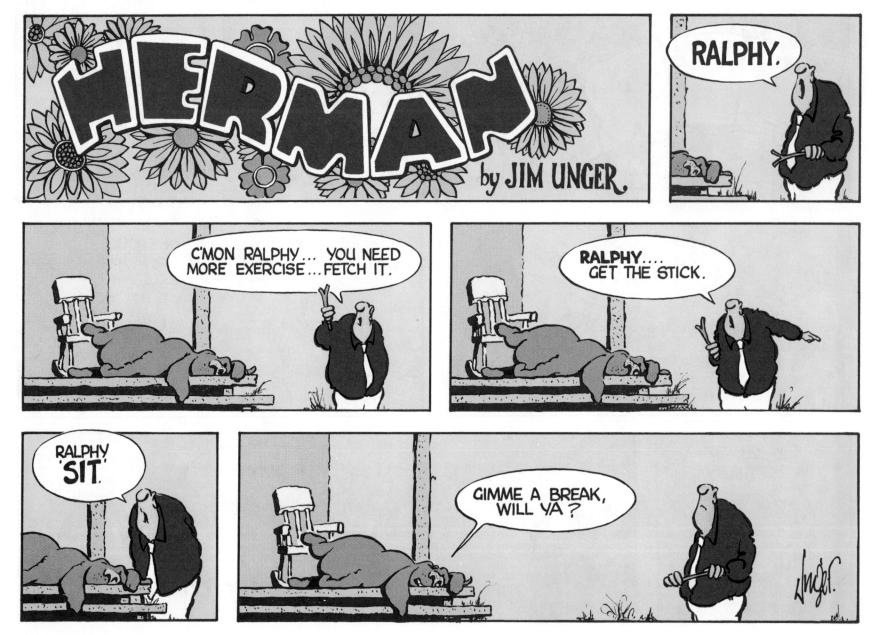

May 1, 1983

May 8, 1983

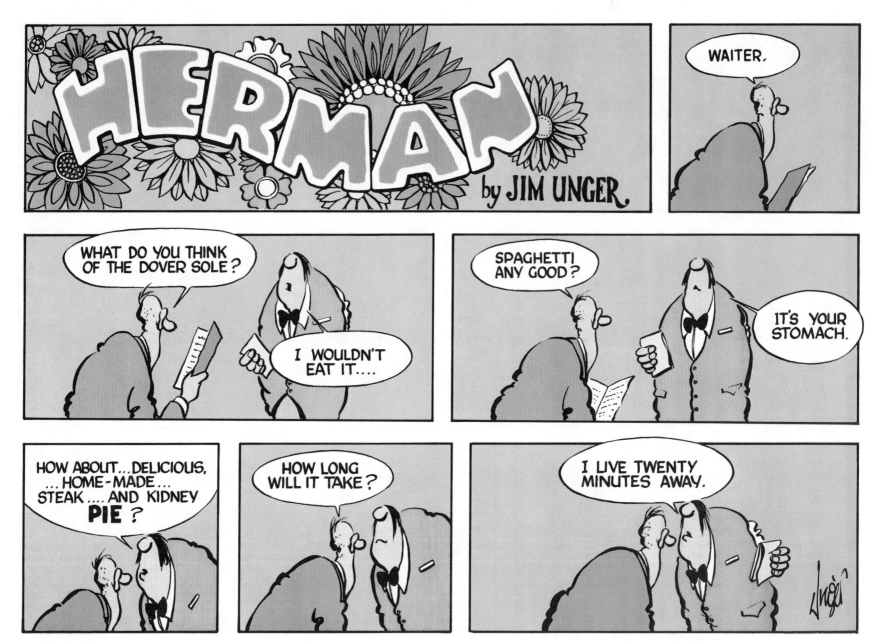

May 15, 1983

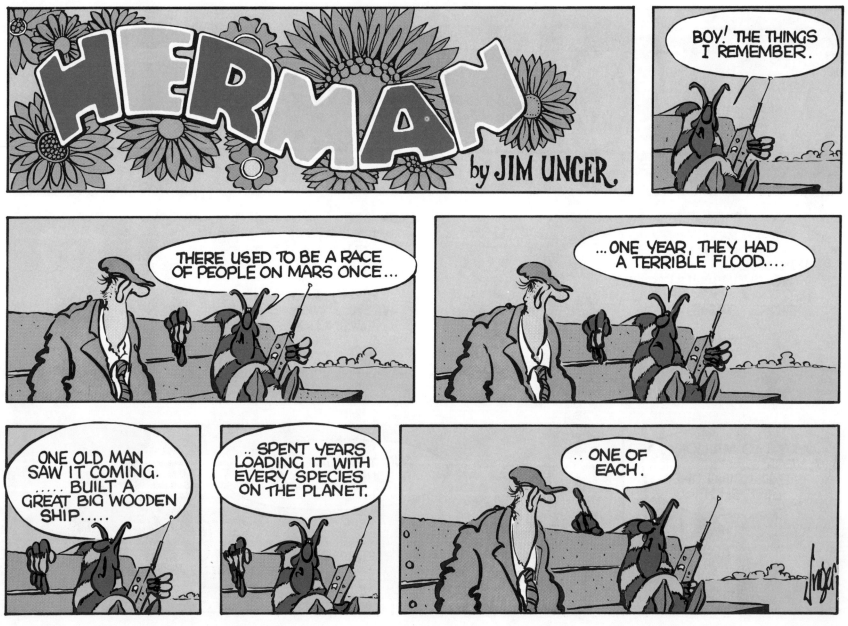

May 29, 1983

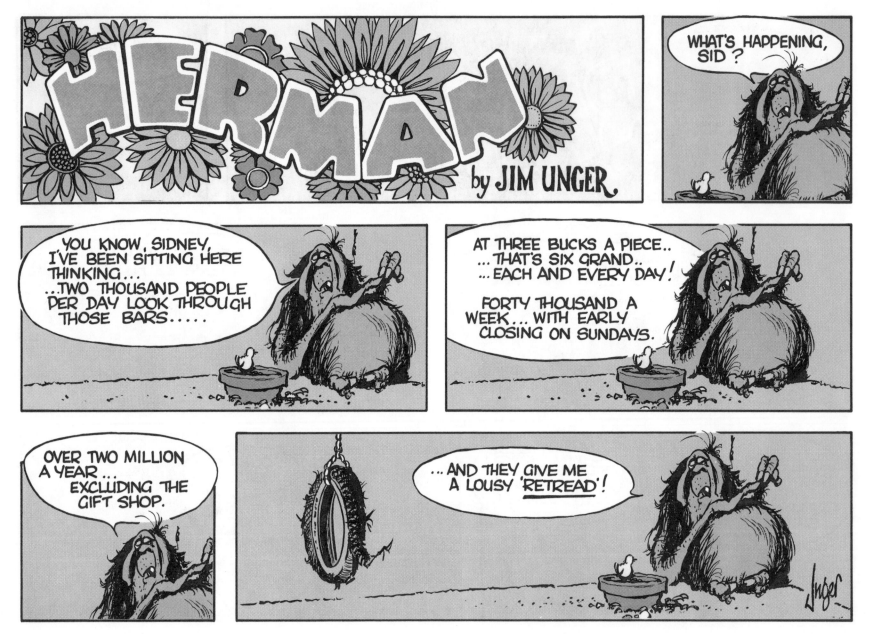

June 5, 1983

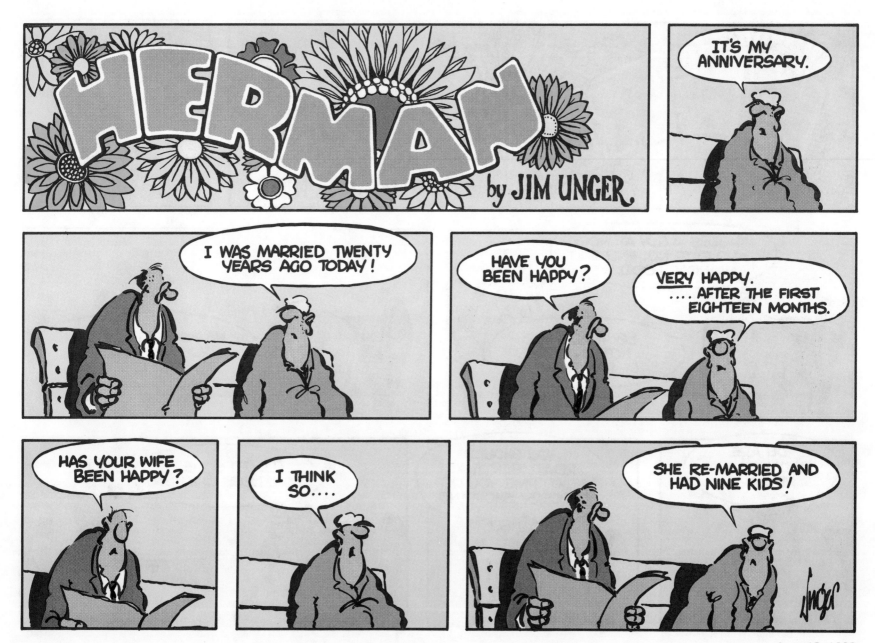

June 12, 1983

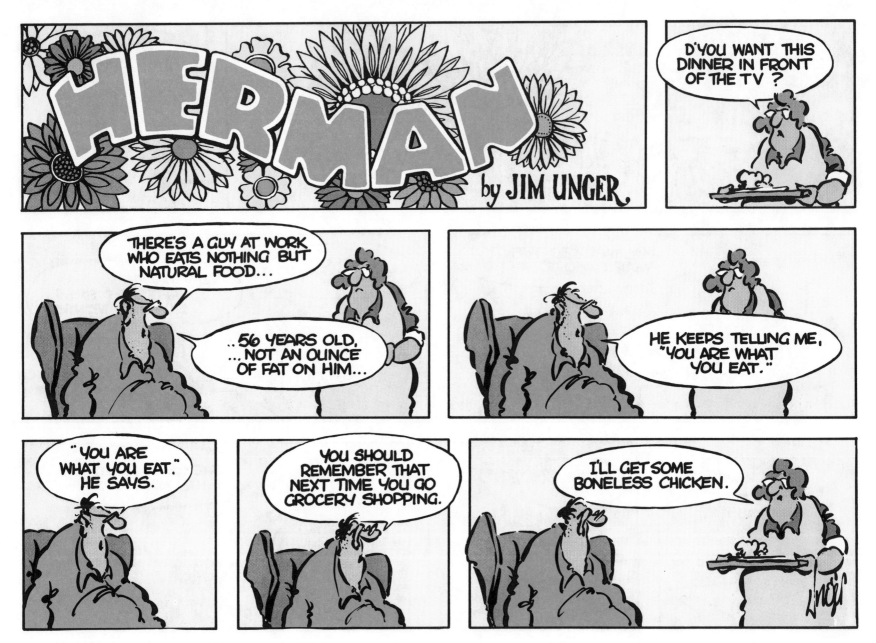

June 19, 1983

July 3, 1983

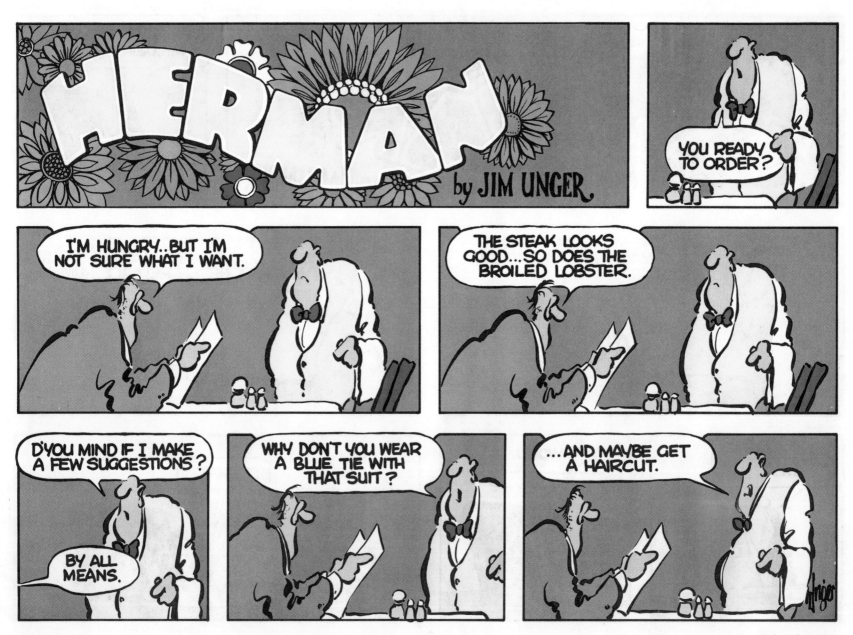

July 10, 1983

July 31, 1983